The Letting Go Workbook

Real-Life Tools:

- Help You Clear the Clutter
- Reclaim Your Time
- Create Space for What Truly Matters

RITA WILKINS, THE DOWNSIZING DESIGNER™

> Your clutter does not define you. Who you are without it—that's where your true story begins.
>
> —Rita Wilkins, The Downsiziing Designer

A Personal Letter from Rita

Welcome, and congratulations!

You've taken the very first step on a life-changing journey, and know this: you are not alone. I'll be right here with you, guiding you as you walk toward a simpler, lighter life with less.

Inside this workbook, you'll discover **10 real-life tested decluttering methods**, plus **3 powerful bonus methods** that have helped countless people let go of what no longer serves them and make room for what matters most.

Think of these methods as your blueprint. They will help you design a home and a life that reflects your values, your dreams, and your next chapter.

This is your invitation to **live more with less**. To experience more freedom, more peace, and more joy by letting go of the excess and embracing what truly matters.

With gratitude and encouragement,

Rita Wilkins, The Downsizing Designer™

About Rita Wilkins,
"The Downsizing Designer"

RITA WILKINS is an interior designer, lifestyle designer, TEDx speaker, and author of the Amazon best-selling book *Downsize Your Life, Upgrade Your Lifestyle*. With over 40 years of design experience, she has helped thousands of people downsize their homes, declutter their lives, and embrace the freedom of living more with less.

After dramatically downsizing her own home and possessions, Rita discovered the life-changing benefits of a minimalist lifestyle—more time for what matters, less stress, and the joy of living intentionally.

She now inspires others to do the same through her speaking events, YouTube channel, online shop, and signature resources like **Rita's Minimalist Essentials Workbook** and **A Journey to Less eBook**.

As Seen In: TEDx, Business Insider, Sixty and Me, Downsizing Designer Blog, and more.

Connect with Rita:

YouTube: Rita Wilkins—The Downsizing Designer **(Subscribe NOW!)**

Newsletter: Join Here for Weekly Tips

Shop: Decluttering & Minimalist Resources

Instagram & Facebook: Rita Wilkins—The Downsizing Designer

Choose What Works for You

You are the expert on your own life—and this workbook is here to support you every step of the way.

DESIGN SERVICES, LTD
4023 Kennett Pike Suite 274
Greenville DE, 19807

The Letting Go Workbook: 10 Proven Decluttering Methods Plus Three Creative Bonuses
Copyright© 2025 Design Services, LTD

All rights reserved. No portion of this book may be duplicated, reproduced, or distributed without written permission from the author. This book may not be stored in a system maintained for retrieval of materials or transmitted in any electronic or digital form such as photocopying, scanning, photographing, and recording.

To request permission to use this material email ritawilkins@ritawilkins.com

Quotations and attributions used in publications, articles, book reviews, and websites do not require written permission from the author.

First Edition: October 2025

ISBN (paperback): 978-1-7334338-3-9
ISBN (ebook): 978-1-7334338-4-6

Contact information: ritawilkins@ritawilkins.com.
Website: www.designservicesltd.com

Printed in the United States of America

Contents
The 10 Core Decluttering Methods

From the Author   v
Introduction   1

Structured & Systematic   3

CATEGORY

1. Method 1: ABCs of Downsizing   5
2. Method 2: Category Method   11
3. Method 3: Priority Method   17

Emotional & Intuitive   23

CATEGORY

1. Method 4: Decluttering by Heart   25
2. Method 5: Room-by-Room Method   31
3. Method 6: Sorting Box Method   37

Creative & Energizing   43

CATEGORY

1. Method 7: Extreme Decluttering Party   45
2. Method 8: Burst Method   51
3. Method 9: One In, Two Out   57
4. Method 10: Hybrid Method   63

BONUS

Bonus Methods   69

1. Declutter Backwards Method   69
2. Layer-by-Layer Method   75
3. Honor It and Let It Go Method   81

Category	Method	One-line Benefit
Category 1: Structured and Systematic	ABCs of Downsizing • Category Method • Priority Method	Visual triage + category focus + plan-first roadmap = fast, confident low-stress decisions for downsizing and organization.
Category 2: Emotional and Intuitive	Decluttering by Heart • Room-by-Room Method • Sorting Box Method	Values-led giving + gentle, steady pace + low-pressure habit = compassionate letting go with sustainable momentum.
Category 3: Creative and Energizing	Extreme Decluttering Party • Burst Method • One In, Two Out	Social sprint + playful prevention = high energy, visible results, and clutter control.

Introduction

Ten Heart-Centered Decluttering Methods for Real-Life Change— Plus Three Bonus Methods

Letting go isn't just about clearing out stuff.
It's about making space for what matters most.

Whether you're downsizing a lifelong home, navigating a major life change, or simply craving more peace in your surroundings, this workbook was created for YOU. With over 40 years of experience helping people create simpler, more intentional lives, I've learned this:

Decluttering is not one-size-fits-all.

- Some people thrive on structure and checklists.
- Others need more emotion and intuition.
- Some want it done quickly. Others want to take it slow.

All of it is okay.

That's why I created these ten flexible, real-life-tested methods—plus three creative bonus methods to help you break through stuck points.

This workbook is your *gentle guide* to decluttering with heart—not just logic.

Inside, you'll find:

- Step-by-step instructions
- Real-life success stories
- Reflective journal prompts
- Practical checklists and emotional tools
- All designed to help you reconnect with what you love—and let go of what no longer serves you.

You don't have to do all the methods. Just start with one.
Let the letting go begin.

Category

Structured & Systematic

Method 1: ABCs of Downsizing

A Visual, Structured Approach to Downsizing Large Items

1. Description

The ABC Method is a powerful, decision-based system for downsizing large items like furniture, decor, and major possessions—especially when preparing for a move like downsizing or moving to a smaller space.

It gives you a clear visual framework to sort your belongings into three easy-to-understand categories:

- **A = Keep**
- **B = Maybe**
- **C = Let Go**

By using sticky notes or tags and working one room at a time, you take the guesswork out of downsizing and reduce decision fatigue. This method is ideal when you need to make smart, quick, and emotionally grounded decisions about what truly fits your next chapter and your new smaller home.

2. Perfect For

- People preparing for a move, downsizing, or rightsizing
- Anyone with a house full of furniture and no idea where to start
- Visual learners who benefit from color-coded systems
- Structure-loving decision-makers who want a fast, effective plan

3. Success Story Example

"We were getting ready to move from our 4-bedroom house to a 2-bedroom apartment. I had no idea how to start, until a friend told me about the ABC Method. I color-coded every big item—furniture, lamps, artwork—with A (keep), B (maybe), or C (let go). Within a few days, I could see what truly mattered to me and what wouldn't fit. It took away so much stress and helped me make decisions with clarity."

— *Maria, 64, downsized after 30 years in the same home*

4. Step-by-Step Instructions

Step 1: Take "Before" Photos

Capture wide-angle shots of each room. This helps document your starting point and makes your progress visible.

Step 2: Tag Each Item Using A-B-C Stickies

- **A (Keep)**: Essential, non-negotiable, loved, and used
- **B (Maybe):** Still useful, but not essential, only if it fits and looks good in your new space
- **C (Let Go):** No longer needed, used, or meaningful

Use colored sticky notes or painter's tape in red (A), yellow (B), and blue (C) for a visual map.

Step 3: Immediately Remove the C Items

Donate, sell, or discard items labeled C right away to free up space and reinforce your momentum.

Step 4: Create a Zone for A Items

Gather your must-keeps into a corner or one side of the room to help isolate and re-evaluate B items.

Step 5: Log A and B Items Into a Simple Inventory

Create a spreadsheet or use pen and paper to record:

- Item name
- Dimensions (for future space planning)
- Quick snapshot/photo
- Keep vs. Maybe status

Step 6: Sketch or Print Your New Floor Plan

Use a sketchpad, graph paper, or digital tool to estimate room sizes in your next space. Don't aim for perfection—just an outline with approximate dimensions will help with furniture layout. Note that a professionally dimensioned floorplan/CAD drawing is best for accuracy.

Step 7: Plot Items in the New Layout

- Start with A items
- Add B items only if they fit and make sense – don't overcrowd your new space
- If they don't? They become C items!

Step 8: Take "After" Photos

Once items are removed or confirmed, take photos to celebrate your progress and clarity.

5. Checklist

- [ ] Take "before" photos of each room
- [ ] Tag each large item using A, B, or C sticky notes
- [ ] Remove C items immediately
- [ ] Group A items together in each room
- [ ] Create an inventory of A and B items
- [ ] Sketch a rough floor plan of your new space
- [ ] Plot A and B items into the plan
- [ ] Take "after" photos
- [ ] Celebrate your clarity and momentum

6. Journal Prompts

1. What does my ideal home feel like—and what doesn't belong in that vision?

2. Why am I holding onto certain B items—and what would it mean to let them go?

3. How do I feel emotionally when I tag something C?

4. Which item surprised me by becoming an A—or a C?

5. What am I making room for in this next chapter of life?

_____
_____
_____
_____
_____

7. Success Tips

- ☐ Use color-coded stickies to make your system visual and easy to follow
- ☐ Measure items before assuming they'll fit in your new space
- ☐ Ask a trusted friend or family member to walk through your B items with you
- ☐ Use painter's tape or cutouts on your floor plan to test-fit furniture
- ☐ Let each completed room fuel your momentum to keep going

8. Before & After Reflection

Before:

"I had furniture and belongings everywhere and no idea where to start. Every room felt like a project I didn't have the energy for."

After:

"The ABC Method gave me structure and confidence. I finally made decisions that aligned with my future, not my past—and that changed everything."

Method 2: Category Method

Declutter by Type, Not by Room

1. Description

If you have *multiples of everything*—too many jeans, piles of unread books, kitchen gadgets you rarely use, or shoes you forgot you owned—the **Category Method** might be exactly what you need.

Rather than bouncing from one room to another, this method focuses your energy on one category at a time, no matter where those items are stored. It's especially helpful if you feel overwhelmed by decision fatigue or tend to get distracted while decluttering.

There's nothing more motivating than seeing real, visible progress in one area. By narrowing your focus to one type of item, you're able to make *clearer, more confident decisions*.

2. Perfect For

- People who have "too much of one thing"
- Those who struggle with decision fatigue
- Anyone who needs a structured, focused approach
- Decluttering in preparation for a move or lifestyle shift

3. Success Story Example

"I never thought I had that many shoes until I put them all in one place. Some still had tags on them! Using the Category Method, I went through every pair—asking, 'Do they fit? Are they comfortable? Will I wear them again?' I ended up letting go of 22 pairs and only kept the ones I truly love and wear. It made me feel lighter—and it made choosing shoes in the morning so much easier."

— *Susan, 68, decluttering before her move to a condo*

4. Step-by-Step Instructions

Step 1: Choose Your Category

Pick one category to begin with—shoes, books, kitchen tools, scarves, bags, coats, etc.

Step 2: Gather All Like Items into One Place

Pull that category from *every* room. Seeing it all together creates clarity and helps eliminate duplicates.

Step 3: Set Up Four Sorting Boxes

- **Keep:** You use it, love it, and would buy it again.
- **Donate:** In good condition, but no longer serves you.
- **Sell:** Valuable items you're committed to selling within 2 weeks.
- **Dispose:** Broken, worn, expired, or unusable.

Step 4: Ask Clarifying Questions as You Sort

- When was the last time I used this?
- Do I need this many?
- Would I buy this again today?
- Does this still suit my lifestyle or values?

METHOD 2: CATEGORY METHOD   13

Step 5: Take Action Immediately
- Trash/Recycle: Remove same day
- Donate: Drop off within 48 hours
- Sell: Set a sale deadline; donate what doesn't sell
- Keep: Put away intentionally and neatly

Step 6: Repeat with a New Category

After celebrating your success, move on to the next. Each category you complete brings more peace and clarity.

5. Checklist

- [ ] Pick your first category
- [ ] Gather all items from every room
- [ ] Set up 4 labeled sorting boxes
- [ ] Ask your clarifying questions
- [ ] Sort every item
- [ ] Take immediate action (dispose, donate, sell, put away)
- [ ] Reflect before moving to the next category

6. Journal Prompts

1. Which categories in my home feel the most overwhelming—and why?

2. What surprised me when I saw everything in one place?

3. What have I learned about my shopping or saving habits?

4. How do I feel now that this category is decluttered?

7. Success Tips

- ☐ Start small—try mugs, scarves, or socks before tackling clothes or books
- ☐ Use a timer—30-45 minutes is a good window to avoid burnout
- ☐ Reward yourself—celebrate with a treat, break, or cozy moment
- ☐ Take before-and-after photos—it's powerful to see your progress

8. Before & After Reflection

Before:

"I had clothes I hadn't worn in years, books I felt guilty about not reading, and shoes I forgot I even owned."

After:

"I can see what I have. I wear what I love. And I'm thinking twice before buying more. The Category Method didn't just help me declutter—it helped me become more intentional."

MY DECLUTTERING PLAN

WEEK 1: LIVING ROOM
Sort books, papers, and décor
(use Keep/Donate/Sell/Dispose)

WEEK 2: KITCHEN
Clear counters, pantry,
expired food, duplicate utensils

WEEK 3: BEDROOM
Clothes, shoes, nightstands,
under the bed

WEEK 4: BATHROOM
Expired products, towels,
extra toiletries

WEEK 6: WHOLE-HOME SWEEP
Quick check to keep only
what I love and use

Method 3: Priority Method

Start with a Plan. Finish with Peace.

1. Description

If you're someone who needs a clear roadmap before you begin, the *Priority Method* might be the perfect starting point for your downsizing or decluttering journey.

This method is about getting *strategic before getting started*. It helps you define exactly what you want to accomplish, why it matters, and how you plan to do it—with realistic goals, timelines, and systems in place.

Rather than bouncing from room to room or stalling out in decision fatigue, the Priority Method empowers you to *start with the end in mind*. It's a thoughtful, goal-driven way to reduce overwhelm, stay motivated, and make measurable progress—even when life gets busy or emotional along the way.

2. Perfect For

- People who love a plan and need to see the big picture
- Those preparing to downsize in the next 3–12 months
- Anyone feeling overwhelmed and unsure where to start
- Project-oriented thinkers who thrive on structure and systems

3. Success Story Example

"Once we decided to move, I felt completely overwhelmed with 30 years of stuff and no idea where to start. Using the Priority Method gave me clarity. I mapped out every room, broke it into weekly goals, and even added our kids to the 'decluttering team.' Seeing our progress on paper each week gave me the momentum I needed to keep going. And it made our eventual move smoother and far less stressful."

— *James, 72, downsized from a 4-bedroom home to a 2-bedroom condo*

4. Step-by-Step Instructions

Step 1: Start with the End in Mind

Write down your "why." Are you downsizing to simplify? Reduce stress? Prepare for a move? Name your motivation.

Step 2: Write Your Specific Goals

Make your objectives time-bound and measurable:

- "Empty attic by September"
- "Declutter entire home by November"
- "Sort and digitize photos by Christmas"

Step 3: Create Your Game Plan

- Map out your home by room or area
- Prioritize which spaces to tackle first
- Decide on your sorting system (Keep, Donate, Sell, Dispose)
- Create a timeline with weekly or monthly milestones

Step 4: Schedule Time on the Calendar

Block out 30–60 minute sessions a few times per week. Treat them like non-negotiable appointments with yourself.

Step 5: Assemble Your Support Team

Who can help you? A spouse, adult kids, a professional organizer, or a tech-savvy friend for selling online?

Step 6: Plan for Motivation

- List five strategies to keep your energy up when motivation dips:
- Uplifting music or podcasts
- Rewards after completing zones
- Watch inspiring transformation videos
- Light a candle and make it cozy
- Pause to reflect and celebrate small wins

Step 7: Track Your Progress

Use a notebook, whiteboard, or spreadsheet to track which rooms you've completed, which are in progress, and what's been sold or donated.

5. Checklist

- [ ] Write down your "why"
- [ ] List your top 3-5 decluttering or downsizing goals
- [ ] Map your home and prioritize areas
- [ ] Choose your sorting system
- [ ] Schedule time on your calendar
- [ ] List your support team
- [ ] Write 5 motivation strategies
- [ ] Create your progress tracker

6. Journal Prompts

1. What does "success" look like at the end of this journey?

2. What are the top 3 areas in my home that cause the most stress or clutter?

3. Who can I ask for help, and how can they support me best?

4. What mindset or habit will I need to let go of to follow through on this plan?

7. Success Tips

- ☐ Break large goals into small milestones (e.g., "sort the junk drawer" instead of "declutter the kitchen.")
- ☐ Celebrate weekly progress—even tiny wins count
- ☐ Be flexible with your schedule; adjust as needed
- ☐ Use visual aids like charts, stickers, or checklists to see momentum

8. Before & After Reflection

Before:

"I felt scattered, overwhelmed, and didn't know where to begin. Everything felt urgent, so nothing got done."

After:

"I had a clear plan. I knew what to do each week. And I could finally see momentum. Having a strategy helped me turn decluttering into something empowering—not exhausting."

Category

Emotional & Intuitive

Method 4: Decluttering by Heart Method

Let Go with Purpose. Give with Love.

1. Description

This heart-centered method focuses on the powerful act of *letting go by giving back*. It's especially helpful in those moments when you're emotionally stuck—holding onto items that are still "perfectly good," or things you spent a lot of money on but no longer use.

Instead of feeling guilty or wasteful, this method invites you to imagine *who could use that item now*. It transforms your decluttering process into an act of kindness, generosity, and emotional release.

You're not just clearing space—you're warming hearts and *giving your belongings a second life*.

2. Perfect For

- People who feel guilty letting go of "perfectly good" items
- Anyone who needs a deeper emotional reason to declutter
- Those who have invested in items but no longer use them
- Purpose-driven givers who want their things to help others

3. Success Story Example

> "I had a closet full of business suits from my corporate years—beautiful pieces I hadn't worn in a decade. I kept thinking 'but I paid good money for these.' One day, I packed them up and donated them to a local Dress for Success chapter. A few weeks later, I got a handwritten thank-you note from a young woman who wore one of my suits to her first job interview—and got the job. I cried. It was the exact closure I needed to finally let go—and the beginning of my decluttering journey."
>
> — *Susan M., age 62*

4. Step-by-Step Instructions

Step 1: Choose a Meaningful Category

Pick an emotionally sticky area—such as formalwear, baby gear, kitchen extras, tools, or books—that you've struggled to let go of.

Step 2: Find a Cause That Matters to You

Choose a charity whose mission resonates. Even better—ask what they currently need most. Examples:

- Dress for Success
- Habitat for Humanity ReStores
- Refugee support organizations
- Women's shelters
- Local libraries or schools

Step 3: Set Up a Donation Zone

Place a box or bag in the room where you're sorting and label it with the name of the organization—it helps reinforce your intention.

METHOD 4: DECLUTTERING BY HEART METHOD   27

Step 4: Declutter with Intention

As you pick up each item, ask:

▷ *Could someone else truly use this now?*
   If yes—place it lovingly into the donation box.

Step 5: Follow Through Promptly

Schedule a drop-off or arrange for pickup within 48 hours. This gives you emotional closure and keeps the momentum going.

Step 6: Connect When Possible

If the organization allows, volunteer, deliver in person, or read stories from recipients. Creating a personal connection can turn decluttering into a mission of love.

5. Checklist

- [ ] Choose a category of items you've struggled to release
- [ ] Find a charity or cause that aligns with your values
- [ ] Ask what they currently need most
- [ ] Set up a labeled donation box or bag
- [ ] Mindfully sort one item at a time
- [ ] Place each item into the box with gratitude and intention
- [ ] Deliver or schedule donation drop-off within 48 hours
- [ ] Acknowledge and celebrate the good you've done

6. Journal Prompts

1. **What feelings come up when I think about letting go of "perfectly good" things?**

2. **Who might need these items more than I do right now?**

3. **What impact could my donation have on someone else's life?**

4. **How do I feel after giving something away with love and purpose?**

5. What am I making space for—physically and emotionally—by letting go?

_____
_____
_____
_____
_____

7. Success Tips

- ☐ Visit the charity's website or location to get inspired
- ☐ Write a short note to the recipient if the organization allows it
- ☐ Remind yourself: keeping something "just in case" might keep someone else from getting it *just in time.*
- ☐ Start small—one bag, one cause, one act of giving
- ☐ Repeat often to build the habit of heart-led decluttering

8. Before & After Reflection

Before

"I felt stuck. I couldn't let go of my things because they were still valuable. I felt wasteful. I kept holding onto them… for what?"

After:

"Letting go felt good. I realized these things could finally fulfill their purpose again—in someone else's life. My space is clearer, and so is my heart."

Method 5: Room-by-Room Method

One Space at a Time, at a Pace That Works for You

1. Description

If you're someone who prefers to take your time, avoid overwhelm, and go at your own steady pace, the Room-by-Room Method may be the perfect fit for you.

This method is ideal if you're *not in a rush*—whether you're not planning to move anytime soon, or you're simply ready to create more breathing room in your home, one space at a time.

It's simple, focused, and satisfying. By working week by week, room by room—or even area by area within a room—you get the *satisfaction of completion* without the stress of tackling your whole home at once.

You'll be amazed at the momentum you build when you finish one space and move on to the next.

2. Perfect For

- People who prefer a calm, steady pace
- Anyone easily overwhelmed by large projects
- Those who want to declutter gradually and intentionally
- Busy people who can dedicate just a few hours each week

3. Success Story Example

"I used to jump around from closet to closet and never seemed to finish anything. The Room-by-Room Method helped me slow down, focus, and feel accomplished. I started with the bathroom, then moved to the linen closet, then the guest room. Each time I finished a space, it gave me more energy to keep going. It was like checking boxes on a to-do list—and I love checking boxes."

— *Linda, 69, recently retired and simplifying at her own pace*

4. Step-by-Step Instructions

Step 1: Pick One Room to Start With

Choose a space that feels manageable—like a bathroom, hallway closet, or spare bedroom. Avoid high-emotion areas (like sentimental storage) in the beginning.

Step 2: Break Larger Spaces Into Zones

For rooms like kitchens or basements, divide the space into smaller chunks—one cabinet, one drawer, or one corner at a time.

Step 3: Stage Four Sorting Boxes

Label each one clearly:

- **Trash:** Broken, worn-out, or unusable
- **Donate:** Good-condition items you no longer need
- **Put Away:** Things that belong elsewhere in the house
- **Repair:** Items worth fixing (zippers, buttons, batteries)

Step 4: Declutter Space by Space

Work methodically and honestly. If you haven't used it, worn it, or needed it in over a year—it's probably time to let it go.

Step 5: Take Action Right After Each Session

- **Trash:** Take it out of the house immediately
- **Donate:** Put it in your car and schedule a drop-off
- **Put Away:** Return items to their proper places
- **Repair:** Set a date to complete tasks or let go of what you won't realistically fix

Step 6: Move to the Next Room When Complete

Pause to enjoy the feeling of a finished space before beginning the next. Let that progress fuel your momentum.

5. Checklist

- ☐ Choose your starting room or sub-area
- ☐ Stage four labeled boxes: Trash, Donate, Put Away, Repair
- ☐ Declutter zone by zone
- ☐ Sort every item into the correct box
- ☐ Take immediate action on each category
- ☐ Celebrate your completed space
- ☐ Move to the next room when ready

6. Journal Prompts

1. **Which room in my home would feel the most satisfying to complete first?**

2. **What emotional or physical blocks have kept me from finishing rooms in the past?**

3. **How do I feel when I walk into a space that's been fully decluttered?**

4. **What would it feel like to take one space at a time—and finish what I start?**

7. Success Tips

- [ ] Use a timer for focused 30-minute sessions
- [ ] Take before-and-after photos—they're incredibly motivating
- [ ] Reuse your sorting boxes from room to room
- [ ] Turn on music, a podcast, or a feel-good movie in the background

8. Before & After Reflection

Before:
"I felt scattered. I'd start decluttering and never finish a room. Everything was half-done and it felt discouraging."

After:
"I started finishing what I started—one room at a time. It gave me a sense of order and momentum I didn't have before."

Method 6: Sorting Box Method
A Low-Pressure, High-Impact Habit That Builds Over Time

1. Description

If you're looking for a simple, low-pressure system that helps you steadily clear out clutter without getting overwhelmed, the **Sorting Box Method** may be just what you've been looking for.

This method is perfect for people who don't have hours at a time to declutter—but want to make real, lasting progress. Its brilliance lies in its *simplicity and consistency*. It transforms your everyday movement through your home into small but powerful opportunities to let go.

It's especially effective for rooms that feel too overwhelming to tackle all at once. Instead of facing the whole mess, you're only dealing with 1–2 items at a time—making it easier to stay emotionally detached and stick with the process.

2. Perfect For

- People who feel overwhelmed by larger decluttering projects
- Busy individuals who want a system that fits into daily life
- Those trying to build a sustainable, lifelong decluttering habit
- Anyone who struggles to start because the job feels too big

3. Success Story Example

"My guest room had turned into a disaster zone. I kept putting it off because I didn't know where to begin. Then I tried the Sorting Box Method. I placed a donate box and a trash bag by the door and promised myself I'd grab one or two items every time I walked past. Within two weeks, the clutter started to disappear. It felt manageable. And best of all, I created a new habit without even realizing it."

— *Mark, 66, retired teacher and part-time volunteer*

4. Step-by-Step Instructions

Step 1: Stage Two Boxes at the Doorway

Label one box **Dispose** and the other **Donate**. Use anything sturdy—bins, baskets, or even bags. Place them by the doorway of the room you want to declutter.

Step 2: Create the Habit

Each time you *enter or leave* that room, place 1–2 items in one of the boxes.

- That's 2–4 items per visit
- Over 7 visits a week, you could remove 14–28 items—effortlessly!

Step 3: Take Action When Boxes Fill Up

- **Dispose Box:** Empty it into the trash or recycling right away, then replace it.
- **Donate Box:** Place in your car and drop off within 48 hours. Replace with a new one to keep the habit alive.

Step 4: Keep the Cycle Going

When one room starts to feel lighter, bring the boxes to another space. You're building momentum and developing a mindset of ongoing release.

Step 5: Let the Habit Sink In

Eventually, you'll start asking:

- "Do I really use this?"
- "Do I really want this in my home?"
- That's the Sorting Box Method at work.

METHOD 6: SORTING BOX METHOD   39

5. Checklist

- ☐ Choose your first room
- ☐ Set up Dispose and Donate boxes by the doorway
- ☐ Commit to removing 1–2 items every time you go in or out
- ☐ Empty and replace boxes as they fill
- ☐ Schedule regular donation drop-offs
- ☐ Celebrate your weekly progress
- ☐ Keep the habit going in new spaces

6. Journal Prompts

1. **What room in my home feels the most overwhelming right now?**

2. **What kinds of items do I keep walking past that no longer serve me?**

3. **How would it feel to make small progress every day instead of waiting for the perfect time to declutter?**

4. **What's the most surprising thing I've learned about my stuff so far?**

METHOD 6: SORTING BOX METHOD

7. Success Tips

- ☐ Start in rooms you use daily—momentum builds faster
- ☐ Use attractive containers if visible boxes bother you
- ☐ Stack the habit with another routine (coffee, feeding pets, etc.)
- ☐ Set a weekly reminder to empty and reset your boxes

8. Before & After Reflection

Before:

"I kept putting it off because it felt like too much work. I never had 'enough time' to declutter."

After:

"I started making small choices every day. Now, my home is lighter, and I didn't have to turn my life upside down to get there."

Category

Creative
& Energizing

Method 7: Extreme Decluttering Party Method

A Step-by-Step Guide to Fast, Fun Decluttering

1. Description

Decluttering doesn't have to be boring—or lonely. The Extreme Decluttering Party turns a dreaded chore into a fast-paced, fun-filled, high-impact group event. Whether you're moving soon, preparing for a renovation, or simply want to jumpstart your momentum, this method helps you tackle a big area in a short amount of time—with help, laughter, and maybe even pizza.

Think of it as the decluttering version of a barn raising: everyone chips in, works hard, and celebrates at the end. You'll be amazed at what you can accomplish in just a few hours with a solid plan and a few trusted friends by your side.

2. Perfect For

- People overwhelmed by large cluttered spaces (garage, attic, basement)
- Those who want fast results and don't mind asking for help
- Anyone prepping for a move or a house sale
- Social declutterers who love collaboration and fun
- Procrastinators who need accountability and a timer!

3. Success Story Example

> "I'd been avoiding our basement for years. When we decided to downsize, panic set in. So I invited my three sisters and a cousin for a Saturday 'Decluttering Party.' I planned snacks, playlists, and even labeled bins ahead of time. We laughed, cried (over old prom dresses!), and filled three carloads of donations. By 5 PM, the basement looked better than it had in 20 years—and we still talk about it as one of our favorite memories."
>
> — *Karen D., age 67*

4. Step-by-Step Instructions

Step 1: Set a Goal and Make a Plan
Decide which space you want to declutter and why. Set a motivating goal (e.g., "Clear out the garage to fit the car before winter").

Step 2: Pick a Date and Timeframe
Choose a 3-4 hour window. Treat it like a real event and block it on your calendar.

Step 3: Assemble Your Team
Invite 3-4 reliable friends or family members. Keep the group small and focused.

Step 4: Prep the Area
Label anything you're *definitely* keeping to avoid confusion. Set up a clean workspace.

Step 5: Assign Roles
Everyone gets a task:

- Sorter
- Boxer/Labeler
- Runner (trash/donations)
- Photographer/Timer

Step 6: Set Up Stations
Create 4 zones:

- Discard
- Donate
- Sell
- Keep

Step 7: Gather Supplies
Boxes, bags, labels, markers, scissors, tape, gloves, cleaning products—and snacks!

Step 8: Post a Timeline and Take Breaks
Outline the schedule and include breaks every 45-60 minutes to stay fresh.

Step 9: Set a Timer and GO!
Start with music and a pep talk. Use a timer to keep things moving.

METHOD 7: EXTREME DECLUTTERING PARTY METHOD

Step 10: Follow Through Immediately

- **Trash:** remove same day
- **Donate:** drop off or schedule pickup
- **Sell/Consign:** label and set deadlines

Step 11: Celebrate!

Host a mini after-party—toast with lemonade or wine, share funny finds, take photos!

5. Checklist

- [ ] Choose space and set a decluttering goal
- [ ] Pick a date and time (3–4 hours)
- [ ] Invite 3–4 helpers
- [ ] Prep the space (label what stays)
- [ ] Assign roles
- [ ] Stage donation and discard zones
- [ ] Gather all supplies
- [ ] Post a timeline with breaks
- [ ] Set the timer and GO!
- [ ] Discard and deliver items that day
- [ ] Celebrate and take pictures

6. Journal Prompts

1. **What's held me back from tackling this space before?**

2. **How did it feel to invite others into my decluttering process?**

3. **What was the most surprising thing we uncovered?**

4. **How did I feel when the timer went off and I saw the progress?**

5. **What can I learn from this experience for future projects?**

_____
_____
_____
_____
_____

7. Success Tips

- ☐ Keep the mood light and the music upbeat
- ☐ Provide drinks and snacks to keep energy up
- ☐ Show appreciation (consider a small thank-you gift!)
- ☐ Don't overthink—trust your gut
- ☐ Schedule another party while the momentum is high!

8. Before & After Reflection

Before:

"I was completely overwhelmed. I had no idea how I'd ever tackle this space, and I kept putting it off because it felt too big to handle."

After:

"I didn't just declutter—I created a memory. I laughed, let go, and made real progress. It reminded me that I don't have to do everything alone."

Method 8: The Burst Method
Declutter Fast in Short, Powerful Sprints

1. Description

If you need a quick win to jumpstart (or restart) your decluttering journey, the Burst Method is your go-to tool. This highly effective, hyper-focused approach uses short, timed "bursts" of energy—15 or 50 minutes—to make fast progress in small, manageable spaces.

It's perfect for people with busy lives, limited energy, or low motivation. Because it's time-bound and focused, it keeps you moving without feeling overwhelmed. Best of all? It works. You'll see results quickly—and that's the kind of motivation that keeps you coming back for more.

2. Perfect For

- People short on time but big on intention
- Anyone overwhelmed by the idea of decluttering the whole house
- Those who love seeing quick, visible results
- People who need a gentle, non-intimidating way to build momentum
- Busy professionals, parents, or caregivers

3. Success Story Example

> "I was feeling stuck. Every time I looked at my kitchen counter, I felt defeated. So I tried the Burst Method—just 15 minutes. I set a timer, turned on music, and went for it. I cleared the counter, sorted the mail pile, wiped down the surface. When the timer went off, I was shocked by how much better the whole room looked. That little burst of success gave me the energy to tackle a drawer the next day. Now I do one burst a day—and I'm seeing real change."
>
> — *Linda M., age 58*

4. Step-by-Step Instructions

Step 1: Choose One Small Area

Pick a contained space that bothers you. It should be doable in one burst (e.g., a drawer, countertop, shelf).

Step 2: Decide on Your Time Burst

- 15 minutes for micro-zones (junk drawer, nightstand)
- 50 minutes for bigger bites (closet, cabinet)

Step 3: Take a 'Before' Photo

Even the smallest transformations are powerful when you can see them.

Step 4: Gather Your Supplies

Have trash bags, donation boxes, labels, markers, and cleaning supplies nearby—no hunting mid-burst.

Step 5: Set Your Timer

Hit start and begin! Don't pause or overthink—just sort and act.

Step 6: Sort into Three Piles

- **Discard**
- **Donate**
- **Keep**

Step 7: Take Immediate Action at the End

- Toss or recycle what's discarded
- Bag and load donations in your car or schedule a pickup
- Return "keep" items to an organized spot

Step 8: Take a 10-Minute Break

Reflect, stretch, and enjoy the shift. Capture an "after" photo for motivation.

Step 9: Repeat (Optional)

Still inspired? Choose the next area and reset the timer. One burst at a time creates major change.

5. Checklist

- [ ] Choose one area to declutter
- [ ] Decide: 15 or 50 minute burst
- [ ] Take a "before" photo
- [ ] Stage all supplies
- [ ] Set the timer and GO
- [ ] Sort into: Discard, Donate, Keep
- [ ] Immediately discard and bag donations
- [ ] Organize what stays
- [ ] Take an "after" photo
- [ ] Celebrate—even small wins matter

6. Journal Prompts

1. **What area of my home stresses me out the most?**

2. **How did I feel before, during, and after my first burst session?**

3. **What surprised me about how much I could do in 15 minutes?**

4. **Where else could I apply this burst method in my daily life?**

5. **What small area can I tackle tomorrow?**

_____
_____
_____
_____
_____

7. Success Tips
- ☐ Keep your timer visible—it keeps you accountable
- ☐ Play energizing music to stay motivated
- ☐ Don't aim for perfect—aim for progress
- ☐ Treat bursts like mini-workouts for your space
- ☐ Stack this habit—try a burst after your morning coffee or before dinner

8. Before & After Reflection

Before:
"I felt paralyzed. I wanted to declutter but didn't know where to start or how I'd find the time."

After:
"In just 15 minutes, I created a win. My space feels lighter, and so do I. I finally see that change is possible—even in small bursts."

Method 9: The One In, Two Out Method
Stop the Clutter Before It Starts

1. Description

This proactive, clutter-prevention method works like a secret weapon: for every **one** new item that comes into your space, **two** must go out. Whether it's a new sweater, gadget, or mug, the "two out" rule forces you to pause, reflect, and choose consciously.

Over time, this shifts your entire relationship with stuff. It helps you **maintain balance**, **shop intentionally**, and keep clutter from creeping back in.

This is the method that doesn't just declutter—it keeps you decluttered.

2. Perfect For

- Anyone trying to maintain a clutter-free home after a big purge
- People transitioning into minimalism or downsizing
- Conscious shoppers who want to be more intentional
- Busy households that accumulate "stuff" quickly
- Anyone tired of feeling like their home is always overflowing

3. Success Story Example

"I used to bring home little things all the time—without thinking. But when I started applying this method, everything changed. I now ask myself: Is this new thing worth letting go of two others? Most of the time, the answer is no. It's helped me shop less, save more, and actually appreciate what I already have."

— *Sharon T., age 62*

4. Step-by-Step Instructions

Set the Rule

Today, commit to following "One In, Two Out" from this point forward. Say it aloud or write it somewhere visible.

Match Items by Category

Bought a new pair of shoes? Let go of two old pairs. New kitchen gadget? Out go two you rarely use.

Take Immediate Action

Place the "two out" items straight into your donation bin, trash, or sell pile. No hesitation. No stash zones.

Track Your Swaps

Use your phone notes or a small journal to record what you're letting go. It builds awareness—and momentum.

Repeat the Practice

Every new thing = two old things gone. You'll notice the shift quickly.

5. Checklist

- ☐ Commit to the 1-in, 2-out rule
- ☐ Apply it starting today
- ☐ Match new item with two items in the same category
- ☐ Let go of the "outs" immediately
- ☐ Keep a simple log or journal
- ☐ Celebrate small wins—your space is staying clear!

6. Journal Prompts

1. **What do I usually bring into my home without thinking?**

2. **How does letting go of two things feel when I bring in one new thing?**

3. **What patterns am I starting to notice in my habits?**

4. **How is my definition of "enough" changing?**

_____
_____
_____
_____
_____

5. **What helps me feel more content with what I already own?**

_____
_____
_____
_____
_____

7. Success Tips

- ☐ Put a sticky note reminder on your front door or wallet: "1 In = 2 Out"
- ☐ Keep a donation box easily accessible at home
- ☐ Make it a household habit—get the whole family involved
- ☐ Combine with intentional shopping rules like 24-hour waitlists
- ☐ Use this method to stay clutter-free between big purges

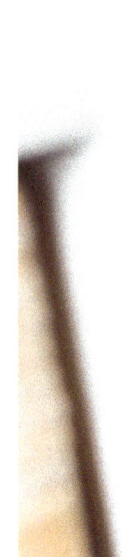

METHOD 9: THE ONE IN, TWO OUT METHOD

8. Before & After Reflection

Before:

"I used to bring home things on impulse and stash them away. Over time, it added up and overwhelmed me."

After:

"Now I pause before every purchase. I only buy what I love—and I release what no longer serves me. My space feels lighter, and so do I."

Method 10: Hybrid Method
Create Your Own Decluttering Blueprint

1. Description

No single decluttering method works for everyone—and that's okay.

The **Hybrid Method** empowers you to **customize** your approach by blending elements from different strategies that fit your personality, lifestyle, and goals. It's about creating a method that's **uniquely yours**—one that energizes you, not overwhelms you.

Maybe you love the visual clarity of the **ABC Method**, the structure of the **Priority Method**, and the emotional grounding of **Decluttering by Heart**. Or maybe you prefer the gentle pace of **Room-by-Room**, paired with quick wins from the **Category** or **Burst** methods.

With the Hybrid Method, *you become the designer of your own decluttering journey.*

2. Perfect For

- People who've tried multiple methods and want to personalize their approach
- Those with unpredictable schedules or shifting energy levels
- Creative thinkers who love to "design their own way"
- Anyone craving flexibility, but still wants a plan

3. Success Story Example

"I kept trying to follow one method at a time, but it never quite clicked. What finally worked was combining the Category Method with a weekly schedule from the Priority Method—and mixing in the ABC stickers for big items. I called it my 'Weekend Warrior Method,' because I do one category every weekend with a glass of wine and music blasting. It made decluttering feel like something I created, not something I dreaded."

— *Elena, 61, creative professional and weekend downsizer*

4. Step-by-Step Instructions

Step 1: Reflect on What's Worked Before

Ask yourself:

- Which methods spoke to me—and why?
- What helped me feel energized, focused, or clear?
- What frustrated me or made me want to quit?

Step 2: Know Your Style & Schedule

- Do you thrive in short bursts or long weekend sessions?
- Do you prefer visual systems, timelines, or checklists?
- Are you more motivated by structure or spontaneity?

Step 3: Mix and Match Your Favorites

Combine 2–3 methods that complement each other. For example:

- **ABC + Category + Priority** = Sort large items first, then small categories, all on a clear schedule
- **Room-by-Room + By Heart** = Go space by space using emotional prompts to guide letting go

Step 4: Name Your Method

Make it personal!

Examples:

- "One Hour, One Drawer" Method
- "Coffee & Categories"
- "Weekend Warrior Decluttering"
- "Two Bags and a Timer"

Step 5: Design Your Game Plan

- What are your weekly steps?
- What tools keep you motivated?
- How will you track progress and celebrate wins?

Step 6: Test It for One Week

Try it. Adjust it. Make it better. Then repeat. Your method evolves with you.

METHOD 10: HYBRID METHOD   65

5. Checklist

- [ ] Identify your favorite methods
- [ ] Write down why they worked for you
- [ ] Reflect on your style, schedule, and energy
- [ ] Combine 2-3 strategies into one custom system
- [ ] Give your method a meaningful or fun name
- [ ] Map out your weekly plan
- [ ] Try it for one week
- [ ] Adjust and keep going

6. Journal Prompts

1. What made certain methods work (or not work) for me in the past?

2. What do I need more of in my process—fun, structure, flexibility, emotional support?

3. What would my ideal decluttering session look and feel like?

4. What would I name my Hybrid Method—and why?

7. Success Tips

- ☐ Embrace trial and error—your system doesn't need to be perfect
- ☐ Personalize it with a playlist, timer, stickers, or treats
- ☐ Visual thinkers: use color-coded notes or charts
- ☐ Treat your method like a living system—it should grow with you

8. Before & After Reflection

Before:

"I felt torn between different methods—none of them worked for me 100%. I kept starting and stopping."

After:

"I realized I didn't need a one-size-fits-all plan. I created something that actually fits *me*. And that's when things finally clicked."

7-DAY DECLUTTER PLAN

DAY 1	Clear shoes and coats
DAY 2	Tidy surfaces
DAY 3	Remove expired food
DAY 4	Sort one category of clothes
DAY 5	Toss expired products
DAY 6	Recycle/shred papers
DAY 7	Celebrate!

THREE BONUS METHODS

Real-Life Tools:

- *Help You Clear the Clutter*
- *Reclaim Your Time*
- *Create Space for What Truly Matters*

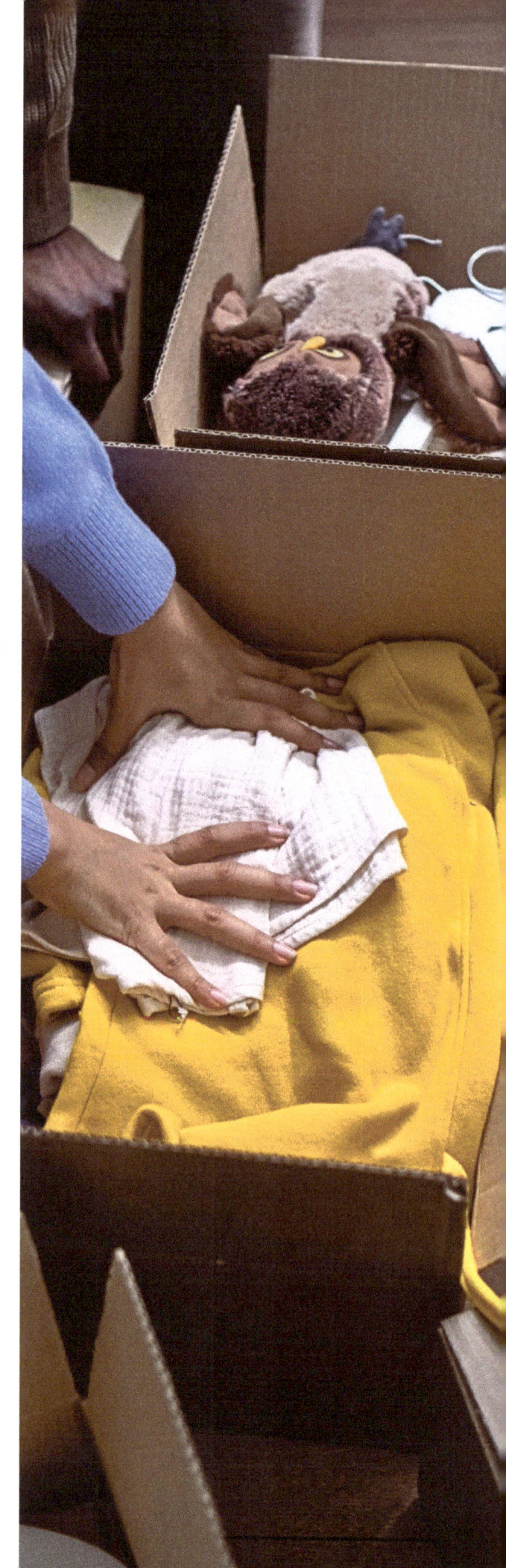

Bonus

Decluttering Backwards

Bonus Method #1: Decluttering Backwards

Flip the Script—Keep First, Then Let Go

1. Description

This out-of-the-box approach is the **opposite** of traditional decluttering. Instead of asking "What should I get rid of?"—you ask "What do I want to KEEP?"

It's a powerful mindset shift that removes pressure and focuses on what truly matters in your next chapter. Ideal for sentimental people or anyone feeling stuck, this method helps you move forward with confidence and clarity.

2. Perfect For

- ▷ People who don't know where to start
- ▷ Sentimental types who feel overwhelmed by decisions
- ▷ Anyone craving a simpler, more empowering framework for letting go

> "When I flipped the process and chose what I truly wanted to take with me to my next chapter, everything changed. It wasn't about what I was getting rid of. It was about what I was keeping."
>
> — Linda, 66

3. Success Story Example

Linda wanted to refresh her bedroom but didn't know where to start. She placed only her favorite quilt, lamp, chair, an area rug in one corner of the room and removed everything else. Those items were easy to part with and made her room, feel lighter and more peaceful than it had in years

Remember: start with what you love and the rest will let go of the others

4. Step-by-Step Instructions

Step 1: Choose a Category or Space

Start with a contained space like a closet, bookshelf, or kitchen cabinet.

Step 2: Start with Your Closet (Test Example)

- Pull out your **keepers**—those high-quality essentials and favorite pieces that make you feel great
- What's left? Sort the rest into four piles:
  - Donate
  - Sell
  - Discard
  - Can't Decide

Step 3: Create a "Maybe Box"

Label and date the box. Put your "can't decide" items inside and store it out of sight for 30 days. Mark your calendar.

Step 4: Closet Review (Midpoint Check-In)

- What have you missed?
- What haven't you worn?
- Are duplicates still taking up space?

Step 5: Day 30—Decide to Decide

Open the "Maybe Box." Sort each item into:

- Keep
- Donate
- Sell
- Discard
- Let go of *"just in case"* thinking. Choose what supports your life now.

5. Checklist

- ☐ Review your keepers
- ☐ Sort everything else into donate, sell, discard, or maybe
- ☐ Place "maybes" in a labeled box for 30 days
- ☐ Revisit and reassess after 30 days
- ☐ Edit your space again

6. Journal Prompts

1. **If I had to pack a suitcase for my next chapter, what would I take?**

   _____
   _____
   _____
   _____
   _____

2. **What do I want in my life and in my space moving forward?**

   _____
   _____
   _____
   _____
   _____

3. **What became easier to release once I focused on what to keep?**

   _____
   _____
   _____
   _____
   _____

DON'T LEAVE too much stuff FOR TOMORROW!

7. Success Tips

- [ ] This is about mindset. Let the question *"What do I want in my life going forward?"* guide every decision.

8. Before & After Reflection

Before:
I was so focused on what I'd have to give up. I felt frozen.

After:
Once I started choosing what I wanted to keep, I felt empowered—not deprived.

Bonus

Layer-by-Layer Method

Bonus Method #2: Layer-by-Layer Method

Declutter Gently, One Emotional Layer at a Time

1. Description

Think of your clutter like an onion—layers built up over time. The **Layer-by-Layer Method** helps you peel back each layer at your own pace, building trust in the process.

This is ideal for those navigating grief, life transitions, or deep emotional attachments. It honors your readiness to let go—without the overwhelm.

2. Perfect For

- People overwhelmed by large-scale clutter
- Anyone recovering from loss, illness, or change
- Sentimental keepers needing time and space

> Each month I peeled another layer, finally reaching his clothing and love letters with peace."
>
> — *Marilyn, 67*

3. Success Story Example

After losing her husband, Carol couldn't face sorting through the home they shared for over 40 years. But she realized she could at least start with an area that wasn't as emotional like the guest room.

She then moved to their study, which allowed her to release another layer of sadness

She was finally able to address her husband's clothing. Little by little each layer lifted the weight of grief until her home felt peaceful again.

Remember: you don't have to do it all at once. Healing and decluttering can happen one gentle layer at a time.

4. Step-by-Step Instructions

Step 1: Choose Your Space

Closet, kitchen, garage—any space that feels manageable.

Step 2: First Layer

Remove obvious trash, expired items, or broken belongings.

Step 3: Second Layer

Let go of duplicates and things you rarely use.

Step 4: Third Layer

Revisit unsure items. Not ready? Set them aside again.

Step 5: Fourth Layer

Face sentimental or emotionally charged items when you're ready.

Step 6: Final Layer

Make clear decisions. Let go with clarity and peace.

Step 7: Celebrate

Each layer is a success. Honor your progress.

5. Checklist

- ☐ Start small
- ☐ Identify and remove the first layer
- ☐ Repeat the process gently
- ☐ Create a memory box if needed
- ☐ Reflect for emotional closure

6. Journal Prompts

1. What layer am I ready to let go of?

2. What emotions lie beneath this clutter?

3. What memory or belief am I holding onto?

4. How do I feel after releasing one layer?

7. Success Tips

- ☐ Set a timer for short, focused sessions
- ☐ Celebrate each round of progress
- ☐ Give yourself grace between layers

8. Before & After Reflection

Before:

I didn't know where to begin. Everything felt too hard.

After:

Now I see decluttering as a process. I feel lighter with every step forward.

Bonus

Honor It & Let It Go

Bonus Method #3: Honor It and Let It Go

Say Thank You. Then Set It Free.

1. Description

Some items carry more than clutter—they carry meaning. This method helps you honor those stories before releasing them. You preserve the memory without carrying the weight.

It's a gentle, respectful process that replaces guilt and obligation with gratitude and peace.

2. Perfect For

- Sentimental keepers and memory holders
- Those holding on from guilt, duty, or identity
- Anyone ready to preserve meaning and move on

> "I honored those years. Now I've let them go—and it feels right."
>
> — Darlene

3. Success Story Example

David found a box of his father's old fishing lures. He held each one in his hand and shared fun stories with his kids and grandkids.

He then kept a few of his favorites and gave a few to his kids and grandkids. The rest he donated to a youth fishing program, passing the joy forward.

Remember: honoring the memory allows you to release the item, but not the love

4. Step-by-Step Instructions

Step 1: Choose a Sentimental Item
Pick one thing or a small group (cards, heirlooms, clothing).

Step 2: Reflect
What does this mean to me? What story does it carry?

Step 3: Honor It
Take a photo, write a note, or say a blessing. Feel the moment.

Step 4: Express Gratitude
Thank it for the role it played in your life.

Step 5: Let It Go
Donate, gift, recycle, or release—whatever feels right.

Step 6: Create a Ritual (Optional)
Light a candle, play music, or write a farewell note to close the loop.

5. Checklist

- [ ] Select a meaningful item
- [ ] Reflect on its meaning
- [ ] Choose how to honor it
- [ ] Release it with love and intention
- [ ] Preserve memory if desired
- [ ] Embrace the freedom

6. Journal Prompts

1. What did this item mean to me?

2. Am I keeping it out of love—or guilt?

3. How else can I preserve this memory?

4. What space will this release create?

7. Success Tips

- ☐ Take a photo and caption it in a digital memory folder
- ☐ Share stories before letting go—it strengthens connection
- ☐ Allow emotions—tears, laughter, and release are all welcome
- ☐ Use rituals: candles, music, prayer, or gratitude moments

8. Before & After Reflection

Before:
I kept this because it meant something once, but I didn't know why I still had it.

After:
I honored its meaning. I preserved the memory. And I let go with love—not loss.

Your Next Step to a Clutter-Free Life
Keep the Momentum Going

You've already taken powerful steps toward a clutter-free, intentional life. Now, let's keep that momentum going with resources that will guide you through the next chapter.

1. **Continue Your Journey—Get Rita's Signature Resources:**

    [Minimalist Essentials Workbook](#)—Your all-in-one guide to decluttering and organizing every area of your home.

    [A Journey to Less eBook](#)—Practical and inspiring tips to help you stay clutter-free for life.

2. **Join the #RitaAndMe Community:**

    Be part of a supportive group of people simplifying their homes and living more intentionally. Share your progress, get inspired, and connect with others on the same path.

    Newsletter: [Join Here for Weekly Tips](#)

3. **Invite Rita to Speak:**

    If you're ready for personal guidance, Rita offers private consultations, downsizing coaching, and event speaking.

4. **Email Rita and Her Team at:** ritawilkins@ritawilkins.com

GIFT FROM RITA: Scan the QR code below for your free

21 Questions: Downsizing? Aging in Place? Or Something Else?